D1168795

SOLVING 25 PROBLEMS IN UNIT DESIGN

How do I refine my units to enhance student learning?

Jay **McTIGHE** | Grant **WIGGINS**

best-selling authors of
Understanding by Design

ASCD Alexandria, VA USA

Website: www.ascd.org
E-mail: books@ascd.org

www.ascdarias.org

Printed in the United States of America. ASCD publications present a variety of viewpoints. The views expressed or implied in this book should not be interpreted as official positions of the Association.

ASCD LEARN TEACH LEAD® and ASCD ARIAS™ are trademarks owned by ASCD and may not be used without permission. Understanding by Design® and UbD® are registered trademarks of Backwards Design, Inc. used under license. All other referenced trademarks are the property of their respective owners.

PAPERBACK ISBN: 978-1-4166-2044-0   ASCD product #SF115046
Also available as an e-book (see Books in Print for the Isbns).

ASCD Member Book No. FY15-6B (April 2015 PS). Member books mail to Premium (P), Select (S), and Institutional Plus (I+) members on this schedule: Jan, PSI+; Feb, P; Apr, PSI+; May, P; Jul, PSI+; Aug, P; Sep, PSI+; Nov, PSI+; Dec, P. For details, see www.ascd.org/membership and www.ascd.org/memberbooks.

Library of Congress Cataloging-in-Publication Data
McTighe, Jay.
 Solving 25 problems in unit design : how do I refine my units to enhance student learning? / Jay McTighe and Grant Wiggins.
   pages cm
 Includes bibliographical references.
 ISBN 978-1-4166-2044-0 (pbk.)
 1. Curriculum planning—United States—Handbooks, manuals, etc. 2. Curriculum-based assessment—United States. 3. Learning. 4. Comprehension.
 I. Wiggins, Grant. II. Title.
 LB2806.15.M3944 2015
 375'.001—dc23
              2014048292

25 24 23 22 21 20 19 18 17 16 15   1 2 3 4 5 6 7 8 9 10

SOLVING 25 PROBLEMS IN UNIT DESIGN

How do I refine my units to enhance student learning?

Want to earn a free ASCD Arias e-book?
Your opinion counts! Please take 2–3 minutes to give
us your feedback on this publication. All survey
respondents will be entered into a drawing to
win an ASCD Arias e-book.

Please visit
www.ascd.org/ariasfeedback

Thank you!

Introduction

Together, we have more than 85 years of experience as professional educators. Much of this experience has involved work on curriculum design, based on a "backward design" approach that we have described in many publications. We developed the Understanding by Design curriculum design framework because we found that traditional lesson and unit plans too often failed to focus on enduring ideas and processes, promote deeper learning, engage students in authentic performance, and equip learners to transfer their learning.

Our design process proposes that effective curriculum is planned backward from long-term aims through a three-stage design process: (1) identify desired results; (2) specify assessment evidence; and (3) detail the learning plan. This backward design process helps to avoid the common twin problems of textbook coverage and activity-oriented teaching in which no clear priorities and purposes are apparent. The process helps teachers help students uncover important ideas of content while promoting meaningful student engagement around outcomes that matter.

Over the years, we have worked with thousands of teachers and design teams and reviewed countless curriculum documents and unit plans. Through our work, we have come to recognize common problems that recur in unit planning. In this book, we identify 25 of those problems, describe indications of each, offer recommendations to correct them, and suggest ways to avoid them in the future.

The book is organized around backward design: the problems are presented in the sequence of the three stages. Since we have found that many problems in unit design are multifaceted, we have referenced related problems and concomitant solutions within this publication. We have also referenced two ASCD publications, *Understanding by Design Guide to Creating High Quality Units* and *Understanding by Design Guide to Advanced Concepts in Creating and Reviewing Units* where more information on unit design can be found. Readers interested in a more thorough treatment of unit design are encouraged to consult these books and related sources.

Problems with Unit Goals (Stage 1)

Problem #1. The unit is overly activity oriented.

When reviewing unit plans or speaking with teachers about them, we frequently see (or hear about) the various activities that their students will do. Not surprisingly, activity-oriented curriculum units are familiar in the visual and performing arts, physical education, and career/technology programs. They are also commonly found in most subjects at the elementary and middle school levels.

The activities listed in these units often seem to be engaging and kid-friendly—fine qualities as long as the activities are purposefully focused on clear and important goals and if they yield appropriate evidence of important learning. We have noticed, however, that many activities are not linked to clear outcomes. In other words, they can be engaging and "hands-on" without being purposeful or "minds-on."

Here's how you can check to see if your unit activities are purposeful and effective:

- Show your learning activities to one or more colleagues and ask them to infer your targeted standards. Can they determine the outcomes that you intended?
- Carefully examine the student work that results from the activities. Does this work provide evidence that students have developed and deepened their understanding of important ideas and can apply their learning in meaningful ways?
- Ask yourself if the time that students spend on specific activities yield significant learning. In other words, is the juice worth the squeeze?
- Ask your students to tell you the purpose underlying the activities. Can they describe the key learning outcomes or are they merely completing the activities as directed?

If you answer "no" to any of those questions, then revise or drop the activities.

When planning a unit, try the following ideas to help focus the learning activities on worthwhile outcomes:

- Consider how students will process the activity. Why? It's typically not the activity that causes deep learning, it's the processing of the activity. Give students ample time to consider the meaning of the activity and ask them probing questions that will prompt them to make connections and generalizations that link to other learning and broad goals.
- Explain the purpose of the activity. If you ask students why they are doing an activity, would they know? As students work on the activity, ask them. Or use exit slips to see if the larger lessons were learned.
- Ask yourself, "What are the enduring, big ideas in this unit?" "What do I want students to really understand about this content?" "How can I best structure activities to help learners come to these understandings?"
- Think of your unit as a story and figure out the moral of it.
- Frame the content of your unit around one or more essential questions.
- Complete this statement: If students really understand this content and have developed the targeted skills, they will be able to _____. Your answer

should help you develop performance assessments that will provide evidence of students' abilities to apply their learning.

(See Wiggins & McTighe, 2011, Module A.)

Problem #2. The unit is coverage oriented.

Covering the content is a time-honored error in planning, teaching, and assessing. It is famously mocked in the movie, *Ferris Bueller's Day Off*, where the economics teacher drones on and on, answers his own questions, and seems oblivious to his bored students. As we are using the word here, coverage is a negative term.

Coverage involves marching through content, topic by topic, without opportunities for students to seriously interact with the material. What is too little appreciated is that coverage, strictly speaking, is thus not really a plan for causing learning at all. It is merely a plan for what the teacher will talk about. The "coverer" naively assumes that teaching is telling and that clear lectures or minilessons lead automatically to learning if the learners will just pay attention.

But given how people learn (by processing what they hear or read in terms of prior learning), the real need in planning and teaching for understanding is to "uncover" the material. To understand is to understand the *why?* the *so what?* and the *how so?* That is, the teacher must routinely stop talking to find out what students are hearing and to give them opportunities to make sense of what is being presented. Any effective plan—even when there is a lot of content to be mastered—must build over time for the students to actively "make meaning" and for the teacher to tease out inevitable learner confusions, questions, and misconceptions that straight lecturing ignores.

A unit plan features excessive or inappropriate coverage if it does not

- Include time for questions, investigations, discussions, or applications of the content. In other words, the plan is only about inputs, not how learner understanding will be achieved.
- Prioritize topics (i.e., each topic seems equivalent to the other topics and is addressed once).
- Allow genuine opportunities for students to ask and pursue in-depth inquiry. In fact, the subtle message is that questions interrupt the flow of coverage.
- Include wait time and genuine opportunities for students to ask questions.
- Deviate from the textbook pages.
- Seek evidence that students have understood what was presented; does not include formative assessments.

Here are some tips on avoiding mere coverage and engaging in uncoverage:

- Pause every 10 to 15 minutes to engage students in actively processing information.
- Include prompts, questions, activities, and formative assessments to determine whether students are "getting" what is being presented.

- Plan the unit around recurring essential questions and key performances that help prioritize the content and focus the learning.
- Code your teaching and learning events using the letters T (transfer), M (meaning making), and A (acquisition) to ensure that the M and T are emphasized, not just acquisition.

(See Wiggins & McTighe, 2011, Module A.)

Problem #3. The unit is test-prep oriented.

The pressures of high-stakes accountability testing have led many well-intentioned school administrators to encourage staff to focus teaching and assessments on those topics and skills that are likely to be tested on standardized tests. Moreover, since standardized tests primarily rely on selected-response (multiple-choice) items, this assessment format is being widely used in unit assessments. The logic is understandable: If we want students to do well on these important measures, they need lots of practice.

However, we caution against limiting the goals of a unit to only those topics and skills that may be found on external tests. To narrow the curriculum in this way undermines the intent of standards and allows important outcomes to slip through the cracks. As an example, Listening and Speaking are included in all English/Language Arts (E/LA) Standards, and yet these are typically not assessed on state/provincial tests. However, Listening and Speaking are underpinnings of Reading and Writing and need to be taught, practiced, and assessed. For example, practice in making arguments in student-led discussion enhances their ability to meet the key standards in E/LA and math on argumentation. Many other valued outcomes, including extended writing, multimedia presentation, use of technology, creative thinking, and teamwork, should be an explicit part of the curriculum and evident within unit plans.

Ironically, the widespread use of narrow, inauthentic assessments and test prep instruction can unwittingly undermine the very competencies called for by Common Core State Standards and 21st Century Skills. It is unlikely that students will be College and Career Ready or equipped to handle the sophisticated work expected in higher education and in much of the workforce if teachers simply march through a coverage of discrete grade-level standards and assess learning primarily through multiple-choice tests of decontextualized items.

Here are specific indicators that unit plans are inappropriately focused on tested content and have a narrow assessment format:

- Learning outcomes that are not featured on standardized tests do not appear in unit goals.
- Unit goals are framed as lists of discrete knowledge and skills.
- Unit assessments mimic the format of standardized tests that primarily use selected-response items (e.g., multiple choice, true or false, matching) often without adequate rigor.

- Learning activities feature lots of decontextualized learning (e.g., skill worksheets) and use of test-prep materials.
- Content is said to be important because students will "need it for the state/provincial test."
- Bored students. Students may be compliant but unenthusiastic about their learning—test prep is not inherently interesting to most learners.

Our tips for averting this problem are straightforward:

- Focus your units around all valued outcomes, not just those things that are easily tested on large-scale tests.
- Frame the content of units around big ideas, core processes, and essential questions to focus on understanding. Think of the more discrete content objectives as the means to larger performance ends.
- Include a variety of unit assessments, including performance tasks and skill checks, not just multiple-choice items, to obtain valid evidence of understanding and transfer.
- Engage students in meaningful learning activities, including inquiry, problem-based learning, critical thinking, research, and developing authentic products and performances.
- Introduce students to the format of standardized tests, but do not fixate on it. The best test prep is engaging and meaningful learning of outcomes that matter. *(See Wiggins & McTighe, 2011, Module D.)*

Problem #4. The unit targets too many standards.

A standard specifies a learning goal—what students are expected to know, understand, and be able to do—and is targeted in unit and lesson planning. A common problem in unit design, however, involves identifying too many standards as goals for a unit. The tendency to identify numerous standards is abetted by electronic unit/lesson planners containing preloaded lists of district, state, and national standards. Such software makes it easy to check off standards. Indeed, we often see unit plans that contain two to four pages of targeted standards! When too many standards are listed as outcomes, the unit loses focus and depth. It is impossible to fully address a multitude of standards in a typical unit that lasts from two to four weeks.

The root of this problem is in the distinction between standards that have been previously taught and will be applied by students within a unit and those standards that are targeted for new learning. Here is an example for a mathematics unit on fractions: *During the unit, students will be adding, multiplying, and dividing fractions.* Most students, however, have already learned the arithmetic procedures of addition, multiplication, and division, so those processes should not be checked as unit outcomes. More generally, prerequisite skill and knowledge should not be identified as unit goals; the unit should target *new* learning.

Our fix for the problem of too many standards is straightforward: Only identify those standards that will be *explicitly* taught *and* assessed within the unit. Here's a practical way to check to see if you have too many standards in a unit plan. Show your planned unit assessments to one or more colleagues and ask them to tell you what standards or outcomes they think are the unit goals. If they can only identify a few, that feedback will enable you to drop the extraneous standards *or* show you that you need to add one or more assessments.

Another technique to check for alignment among chosen goals, assessments, and instructions is to code the outcomes for your unit plan. For example, choose codes for standards (E/LA 3.4) or S1, S2 (for skill #1, #2). Then, match the appropriate coded outcomes with your unit assessments and major learning activities. If you have listed standards that cannot be matched, you have two options: (1) drop them since they are not being taught or assessed, or (2) add to your assessments and/or revise your lesson plans to include them.

See Problem #1 for a related solution.

(See Wiggins & McTighe, 2011, Modules C, D, I.)

Problem #5. The unit lacks understanding-based goals.

When designing units, teachers are encouraged to identify the big ideas that they want their students to understand, in addition to the more specific knowledge and skills they need to learn. The understandings reflect the specific insights, inferences, or conclusions that students should attain. They are responses to questions such as, "These are the facts, but what do they *mean*?" "You have used these skills, so what do you now understand about their effective use?" The phrase, *coming to an understanding,* is suggestive of the idea that an understanding is a thoughtful inference made by the learner. It is a conclusion—using facts and experience—a "moral of the story" of the unit, like the morals of Aesop's Fables.

Yet a quick look at many unit plans reveals that the goal statements only identify knowledge and skill outcomes. This problem is evident in units that

- Give a long list of facts and skills without higher-order goals related to understanding concepts, application of learning, or inquiry.
- Offer a list of sub-standards focusing only on low-level objectives, rather than on the top-level (i.e., more complex) standards.
- Use only a word or phrase to state the topic ("understand metaphors" or "understand the Civil War"), not a specific understanding sought about the topic.
- List a skill or process rather than an understanding about it; for example, rather than "understand how to write a persuasive essay," state an understanding *about* persuasive writing. For example, "Effective persuaders select examples and use language suited to their target audience."

To address this concern, we highly recommend using a unit template and design process that prompts teacher-designers to consider more than just knowledge and skill. At its essence that is what the Understanding by Design Unit

Template offers: a tool for avoiding the common habit of overlooking understanding-related and other higher-order goals in unit design.

Here are some other tips on identifying and writing more intellectually robust unit goals:

- Identify the transferrable big ideas that you want students to come to understand about the content.
- Begin with the sentence stem, *I want students to understand that* _____ because it forces you to write a statement that summarizes an inference that learners should draw.
- Seek specificity and depth. If the understandings are vague or superficial, ask yourself: "Why is this important?" "Why does this matter?" "What's the transferable idea that can apply in multiple settings?"
- Frame the content of the unit with essential questions that point toward conceptually larger ideas and processes.
- Answer this question: What does an expert performer understand about this (skill or process) that a novice or an unskilled performer does not?
- Think about possible or predictable misunderstandings. What is the real understanding about this concept or process?
- Focus the unit around performance tasks that call for transfer applications. Then, plan backward from those to identify the requisite knowledge, skills, and understandings.

(See Wiggins & McTighe, 2011, Modules E & F; Wiggins & McTighe, 2012, Module L.)

Problem #6. The unit goals are not clearly related.

As the word *unit* signifies, a key goal in unit design is coherence of learning. This unity must be visible to students, not just to teachers who are already familiar with the content. In some units, we see a mish-mash of unrelated goals with no apparent connection or logical flow to learners, making learning far more difficult and less engaging than it needs to be.

Unit goals lack unity and coherence when they

- Do not naturally fit together under unifying ideas or meaningful applications. For example, a unit may include a set of vocabulary words that are tangential to the key topics, skills to be learned, and texts to be read.
- Attempt to encompass too many standards, perhaps selected from grade-level standards documents and kept in the order presented in those documents.
- Are not prioritized by knowledge, skill, inquiry, or application of learning.

The best way to help learners see connections among goals is through the use of themes, essential questions, and/or recurring applications in which the content is clearly needed and woven together in performance. Here are some tips for helping students perceive greater coherence and unity among your unit's goals:

- Frame your unit by first considering desired performance results. For example, what do you want students to be able to do with everything they will learn during the unit? Then, think like a coach and plan backward to consider what knowledge, skills, and strategies the players will need for effective performance. When you use this approach to framing a unit, it is easier for students to see how specific lesson objectives work together and contribute to worthwhile unit goals.

- Use big ideas (themes, issues, problems, or authentic tasks) and essential questions to structure your unit. Then, see if the identified learning goals fit naturally under these important concepts. If not, reconsider the content and skills being targeted.

- Make a concept web of all the unit goals to see the various points of connection. If there are goals that do not fit, then they might best be taught in other units.

- Prioritize the unit by making it clear to learners how the facts and discrete skills are subsumed under the more complex performance task(s) to which they relate. In other words, help students distinguish the means versus the ends.

(See Wiggins & McTighe, 2011, Module E.)

Problem #7. Essential questions—aren't.

We encourage teachers to frame the content they teach around essential questions. Too often in unit plans, however, we see questions that have been identified as essential, but are really convergent questions with correct answers.

A solution to this problem begins with an understanding of the characteristics of an essential question. Essential questions

- Are inherently open-ended and do not have a single, correct answer.
- Are intellectually engaging, intended to spark interest, inquiry, higher-order thinking, discussion, and debate.
- Point toward important, transferable ideas and processes within and across disciplines.
- Raise new questions and spark further inquiry.
- Require support and justification, not just an answer.
- Recur productively over time and can and should be visited again and again.

Questions that meet all or most of these criteria qualify as essential. Their aim is to stimulate thought, to provoke inquiry, and to spark more questions, including thoughtful student questions. By tackling such questions, learners are engaged in making meaning about important ideas and processes.

With good intentions, teachers often err in assuming that an essential question points toward important content outcomes. In these cases, the questions are guiding questions that are intended to steer students toward definite answers. Although guiding questions are certainly useful for helping teachers achieve specific content goals, they are not open-ended or provocative enough to spark sustained student inquiry and argument, which is the intent of an essential question.

Here's a practical test to check on the "essentialness" of a question: Could you post this question on your classroom wall or board and productively use it *throughout* the unit (as opposed to a question that you might ask once or twice)? A more formal solution to this problem is to subject your proposed unit questions to the list of characteristics of essential characteristics. Do they meet these criteria? If not, you can try to expand the questions.

(See Wiggins & McTighe, 2011, Module F; Wiggins & McTighe, 2012, Module L.)

Problem #8. Unit goals fail to distinguish means versus ends.

A common mistake in unit writing is to identify goals that reflect only discrete facts and skills—low-level, bite-sized objectives. The demand that students learn a fact or a skill is not a goal, strictly speaking. Facts and skills are the *means* to the larger and more complex learning goals involving understanding and performance. Units written with the means, not the end, in mind:

- Focus on discrete facts and isolated sub-skills rather than on (a few) complex performance goals that require the facts and skills.
- Break down complex ideas and processes into simplistic bits and pieces that do not add up to rich and flexible understanding and fluent performance.
- Ask for recall of information rather than on understanding and transfer.

Athletics present a clear example of the distinction between a complex performance goal and discrete objectives that focus only on knowledge and isolated skills. The goal of soccer or basketball is not to master a long list of discrete skills. The skills are necessary but insufficient—they are means but not end. The goal is to get better at the game (a complex performance), not merely to master a set of drills.

The same logic applies to all subjects. Mastery is more than just the learning of isolated bits. Mastery refers to the effective use of knowledge and skills in complex situations. Practically speaking, this means designing units around complex performance goals that require understanding and transfer; that is, knowing how and when to use and adapt content to meet performance demands.

Here are some tips for ensuring that you have complex, transfer-focused goals in your unit:

- Focus on long-term performance goals (e.g., Anchor Standards for E/LA or the Practices Standards for mathematics and science). Then frame unit goals "backward" from these.
- Distinguish between short-term objectives and long-term performance goals (or equivalent phrases), when identifying unit goals.
- Ask yourself: "If the content is the means, then what is (are) the performance end(s)?" "If this is a 'drill,' then what is 'the game'?" Use the answer(s) as the primary goal(s) for your unit.
  (See Wiggins & McTighe, 2011, Modules C, E, I.)

Problem #9. Failing to distinguish between knowledge and skill objectives.

Knowledge objectives specify what we want students to *know*—facts, key vocabulary, and basic concepts. Skill objectives are procedural in nature—they state what we want students *to be able to do*. Examples of skills include drawing a 3–D view of an object or dribbling a basketball. Sometimes unit designers incorrectly identify knowledge objectives as skills. This problem is evident when knowledge objectives for a unit are preceded by verbs and listed as skills.

Here are examples of knowledge outcomes listed as skills:

- Students will be skilled at explaining the contributions of key historical figures.
- Students will be skilled at categorizing types of rocks.
- Students will be skilled at identifying the flaw in an experimental design.

These three examples actually identify knowledge objectives. Students are expected to *know* contributions of key historical figures, characteristics of different types of rocks, and the elements of an experimental design. The verbs may suggest ways of *assessing* this knowledge, but the actual learning outcomes are knowledge based.

Why does this distinction matter? Clarity about unit outcomes influences instruction and assessment: knowledge and skill objectives are taught and assessed differently. For example, when teachers want students to learn and remember factual information, they can present that information using a lecture or presentation, have students read or view it, offer a useful mnemonic, and have students review it to commit the knowledge to memory. Skill instruction is different: When teaching skills, teachers typically model the skill, have students practice and refine the skill while providing feedback, and continue the practice in more complex/new situations until automaticity is achieved. *("I do, you watch. You do, I watch.")*

The proper assessment of knowledge and skill is also different. Factual knowledge can be readily assessed through objective questions or test items with "correct" answers. After all, knowledge is binary—the student either knows it or not. In contrast, skills are most appropriately assessed through performance—by watching the student performing the skill or assessing the products of their performance (e.g., a drawing). Rather than being right or wrong, a skill performance is judged according to a proficiency scale or continuum ranging from flawed/unskilled to expert performance.

In the logic of backward design, clarity about the nature of the learning objectives informs all other aspects of the unit plan and results in more effective learning.

(See Wiggins & McTighe, 2011, Module E.)

Problems with Assessment Evidence (Stage 2)

Problem #10. The proposed assessments do not provide appropriate evidence for all unit goals.

Validity is about the logical alignment of goals and evidence: Given the goal, does the proposed assessment really measure it? Or is the assessment really assessing something other than was intended? An assessment provides a valid measure when performance on a (specific) assessment lets us draw sound inferences about achievement of a (broader) goal.

A familiar problem in unit design is evident when the assessments do not provide appropriate evidence for *each and every* goal identified in Stage 1. Appropriate assessments provide evidence that enables valid inferences about a student's attainment of a targeted goal. For example, only having a written test of driving ability would be an inappropriate assessment because someone could "pass" a paper-and-pencil test on the knowledge of rules of the road without being able to skillfully operate a car on the highway.

Here are common indicators of invalid unit assessments:

- Allow for success on the task for reasons other than achieving the targeted learning. For example, a student receives a high score on an oral presentation, more for wit and articulateness than because of deep understanding of the topic.

- Allow for failure or poor performance at the task for reasons that are tangential to the targeted goals and are more closely related to other skills and knowledge. For example, a shy student is uncomfortable talking in front of groups, even though she understands the topic fully (where the task was meant to assess understanding, not public speaking).
- Use items, questions, or tasks that are unfair because they do not appropriately reflect the prior learning and/or the targeted outcomes.
- Use of items, questions, or tasks that are too narrow and thus fail to sample the entire range or types of challenges related to the goals being assessed.
- Inclusion of items, questions, or tasks were practiced in class such that the assessment is really measuring recall rather than genuine understanding.

There are three practical ways to check for invalid unit assessments.

1. Use the two-question test to check for assessment validity:

- Could a student pass your test or perform the task in a way that meets your performance criteria/rubric, but not convincingly demonstrate the targeted knowledge, understanding, and/or skill proficiency?
- Could a student do poorly on your test or not meet your performance criteria/rubric, yet have attained

the targeted knowledge, understanding, and/or skill proficiency?

If the answer to either question is "yes," then one or more of your assessments is likely to yield invalid results and fail to provide the appropriate evidence.

2. Conduct an "alignment check." Here's how it works: Identify the learning outcomes for your unit (from Stage 1), including standards, understandings and essential questions, knowledge, and skills. Specify the assessments that you will use to determine the degree to which students have attained these outcomes. Next, show your planned unit assessments to your colleagues and ask them to identify the unit goals. If they can only identify a few of your desired results, that feedback signals that there is not yet a tight alignment between your assessments and your goals.

3. Code the outcomes for your unit plan, for example, use standard numbers (E/LA 3.4) or S1, S2 (for skill 1, skill 2). Then, match the appropriate coded outcomes with your unit assessments and major learning activities.

Once you recognize the problem is that not all listed goals are being appropriately assessed, you have three options:

1. Drop any unit goals that are not being explicitly assessed.

2. Add appropriate assessments to match the goals for which assessment evidence is not yet evident.

3. Modify the existing assessments to ensure that they provide appropriate evidence of the targeted goal(s).

See Problems #1 and #4 for related solutions.

(See Wiggins & McTighe 2011, Module G; Wiggins & McTighe, 2012, Module M.)

Problem #11. There is insufficient evidence of learning to ensure reliable assessment.

Reliability is about patterns of results in assessment. When we say the evidence is *reliable*, it means that we have a large enough sample or set of data to give us confidence that the results reflect the true achievement of the student, not an outlier. Unreliable results involve having too much error based on too little evidence to say with confidence that a summary judgment reflects a stable result or pattern.

Here are indicators of unreliable assessments:

- Test scores and results vary widely for individuals and/ or the whole class over time.
- Key outcomes are measured with only one test item or performance task.
- You have a hunch that the most recent assessment result does not accurately reflect students' true level of ability or achievement.

Notice that reliability is quite different from validity. In any sport, for example, the game result is always valid because the game is the desired performance. But a single result is unreliable: even weak teams may win one and dominant teams sometimes lose. Alas, in schooling, we often make the mistake of over-generalizing from one result. We evaluate one quiz, paper, or performance task and are prone to draw a sweeping conclusion from it about a student's overall achievement.

Thus, a practical maxim for enhancing reliability comes from our legal system: Assume the student is innocent of achieving or not achieving a goal unless proven guilty by a preponderance of evidence. Practically speaking, this means that the only way to achieve reliable results is through varied, multiple, and spaced assessments of the same key goals or standards. Redundancy in the assessments is a good thing, especially for key outcomes such as anchor standards, mathematical and scientific practices, and authentic performances.

Here are other tips for achieving greater reliability in our assessments:

- Use a parallel quiz, writing prompt, or exit ticket for every test, task, or project to get further information about the same goals for each student.
- Ensure that key outcomes (e.g., writing in various genres, critical thinking, research) are assessed multiple times during the unit, as well as across units, to gather a reliable collection of evidence.
- Triangulate the assessments—use several different types of assessments to ensure that the pattern of results holds true across events and kinds of challenges.

(See Wiggins & McTighe, 2012, Module M.)

Problem #12. Performance tasks are contrived and inauthentic.

Some curriculum units contain performance tasks that may involve application but are not authentic. Certainly, not all unit performances need to be authentic. Responding to an academic prompt (e.g., What is the main idea of the text?) or demonstrating a discrete skill (e.g., factoring in mathematics) calls for performance, but does not reflect real world application—nor does it need to. However, we encourage teachers to include at least one authentic task in major units.

A performance task may be considered authentic if it reflects the way in which people in the world outside of school must use knowledge and skill to address various situations where expertise is tested or challenged. Authentic tasks typically include a goal (e.g., solve a problem, analyze an issue, conduct an investigation, communicate for a purpose), and a target audience and realistic constraints (e.g., a time schedule, budget). These tasks yield tangible products (e.g., a position paper, a poster, a 3-D model) and performances (e.g., an oral presentation, a skit, a demonstration) that are valued in the wider world.

It is easy to tell if performance tasks are contrived. Indeed, students are often quick to let us know. Here are a few indicators:

- Hear older students say "This is stupid." "Are you kidding me?"
- Get questions from students, "Why are we doing this?" "Who would ever do that?"

- Watch students as they work: Are they genuinely engaged in the performance? Are they trying their best? Are they proud of their accomplishments? Inauthentic work typically involves only extrinsic motivation.
- Ask yourself, "Does anyone outside of school do this or produce such a product?"
- Show the task to a few colleagues and ask them to tell you what learning outcomes they think are being taught and assessed through this task.
- Ask yourself, "Is this task really worth the time and effort?"

Establishing an authentic context for a performance task has value from an assessment perspective (not just a motivational one) because it enables us to see evidence of understanding and transfer. When students are able to apply their learning thoughtfully and flexibly under realistic conditions, true understanding is demonstrated. An additional benefit to authentic tasks is that students are more likely to see value in what they are being asked to learn when purpose, relevance, and a realistic context are established.

One suggestion for enhancing the authenticity of performance tasks is by framing them using the G.R.A.S.P.S. elements—(1) a real-world Goal; (2) a meaningful Role for the student; (3) authentic (or simulated) Audience(s); (4) a contextualized Situation that involves real-world application; (5) student-generated Products and Performances;

and (6) the performance *Standards* (criteria) for successful performance.

(See Wiggins & McTighe, 2012, Module M.)

Problem #13. Performance assessment tasks are not worth the effort.

Performance tasks are intended to engage students in applying their learning while enabling teachers to assess students' understanding and proficiency. The best performance tasks are authentic; that is, they are set in a meaningful, real-world context and result in a tangible product (e.g., a diagram, essay, video) or performance (e.g., oral presentation, debate, dramatic enactment). Performance tasks are often engaging for students, serving as rich learning experiences as well as robust assessments. Their open-ended nature can allow student choice and encourage creativity.

We have witnessed instances, however, in which well-intentioned teachers develop tasks that may be authentic but prove to be difficult to implement or not worth the effort when all is said and done. This problem is evident when the preparation of products or performances requires an inordinate amount of time and distracts from the fundamental purpose of the task (e.g., making costumes for a role-playing task, decorating posters for a science project, getting bogged down by technology glitches when preparing a multimedia presentation). A teacher friend of ours offers a wise aphorism: With performance tasks, the juice must be worth the squeeze!

We have several recommendations for avoiding the problem of inefficient or cumbersome tasks:

- Specify the key qualities that characterize successful performance *relative to the unit goals* being assessed, and use these as your key evaluative criteria. Too often, evaluative criteria or rubrics focus on "surface features" (e.g., neatness, creativity, number of words) rather than on the most salient traits linked to standards or goals. Once you have determined these key traits, review the criteria or rubric(s) with students *before* they commence work on their products or performances. By building and sharing rubrics around the key criteria, you signal students to concentrate on key qualities so as to avoid wasting time on superficial elements.

- Apply the two-question test (also shown in Problem #10) to check for assessment validity:
  - Could a student pass your test or perform the task in a way that meets your performance criteria/ rubric, but not convincingly demonstrate the targeted knowledge, understanding, and/or skill proficiency?
  - Could a student do poorly on your test or not meet your performance criteria/rubric, yet have attained the targeted knowledge, understanding, and/or skill proficiency?

- If the answer to either question is "yes," then one or more of your assessments is likely to yield invalid results and fail to provide the appropriate evidence.

- Try the task yourself and develop one or more sample responses. Nothing reveals potential weaknesses in performance tasks more than actually trying the task (or asking a colleague to do so) and testing your evaluative criteria/rubric(s) on the products. You will quickly find out if the directions are clear, the rubric is aligned with the unit goals, and the task is worth the time and effort.

See Problems #10, #11, #12 for related solutions.

(See Wiggins & McTighe, 2012, Module M.)

Problem #14. Performance tasks or projects may not yield valid assessment evidence for *individual* students.

Students often find authentic, hands-on projects and performance tasks interesting and motivating, as noted in Problem #13. However, the very things that engage can also compromise the validity of assessments. Unlike a traditional test that is typically completed individually in a short time frame, performance tasks occur over time. Thus, students may have many opportunities to help each other and teachers may provide varying levels of guidance and feedback. When the tasks involve student collaboration on a single product or performance, the problem is enhanced.

In these cases, the validity of individual results is easily compromised: The greater the collaboration and teacher input, the less we know for sure about what each student really understands and is able to do on his or her own. More generally, any performance task can be invalid for individual students if or when there is no way to precisely identify each student's skill, knowledge, and/or understanding.

An assessment task may not provide valid assessment evidence for individual students if it:

- Involves significant conversation and a group project, so that the work reveals only collective achievement, not individual achievement.
- Requires constant interaction among the students and with the teacher, so there is a lack of evidence about independent and individual achievement for each student.

Here are some tips for achieving appropriate assessment evidence for each student when using a complex task or project:

- Redesign the task so that it includes at least one individual product for every student.
- Use an individual parallel assessment (e.g., test or minitask) for every task or project on the same content.
- Use a rubric to assess the effectiveness of teamwork if collaboration is a targeted outcome—and use a separate rubric tied to the content outcomes.
- Include a rubric that describes the degree of student autonomy, if students receive help during the task.

(See Wiggins & McTighe, 2011, Module G; Wiggins & McTighe, 2012, Modules J & M.)

Problem #15. The evaluative criteria or rubric(s) are invalid.

Units that contain open-ended performance tasks or projects require an appropriate set of evaluative criteria or rubrics for judging student performance. In some instances, the criteria or rubric(s) attached to the tasks do not align with the goals and will therefore lead to invalid assessment. This problem is especially evident when the evaluative criteria or rubric(s) focus on superficial features (e.g., number of words, neatness, number of errors) or arbitrary requirements (e.g., five paragraphs in an essay) at the expense of those traits most aligned to the standard(s). Another example of this problem is seen in "count on your fingers" rubrics, where a research paper receives a *4* if there are four sources cited and a *3* for three sources. In this case, the performance rating is based on the number of sources that are easy to count, with no reference to the quality, contribution, or appropriateness of the sources.

There are several ways of reworking the assessment to ensure the associated evaluative criteria and rubrics are appropriate. When planning unit assessments, we recommend starting with a focus on the unit goals (i.e., the targeted standard/outcome in Stage 1), *not* on the particulars of the task or project (Stage 2). Given the unit goal(s) being assessed through the task, identify the key qualities associated with successful performance and understanding. In a mathematics task, for example, we might look for *effective application of concepts, sound mathematical reasoning, accuracy of computation,* and *detailed explanation of the solution process.* These are valid criteria since a performance, to be sound, must meet these criteria.

Once these key traits are determined, we can then flesh out a more detailed rubric by describing varied *degrees* of understanding, proficiency, or quality on a performance scale. For example, here is a rubric for assessing student understanding in terms of the quality of argumentation:

1. The work is unusually well-reasoned, accurate, and fully supported. All key claims are supported by appropriate, thorough, and compelling evidence as well as by sophisticated and sound reasoning. Important alternative views are presented through the most salient counterarguments and counterexamples and addressed fairly and fully.

2. The work is generally well-reasoned, accurate, and supported. There may be minor errors in reasoning and/or evidence but they detract minimally from the overall quality of the argument(s). Alternative views are presented through counterarguments and counterexamples.

3. The work contains some flaws, with errors and/or gaps in logic or evidence. There is an argument, but some important claims are made without sufficient or appropriate backing. There may also be gaps in reasoning where a conclusion is reached without a complete chain of logic to support it. Alternative views may be presented through counterarguments and/or counterexamples but the treatment may be cursory or ineffective.

4. There are significant and noticeable weaknesses in the reasoning and/or evidence offered. Key claims may be merely stated rather than argued and the conclusion is unwarranted. Little or no serious consideration of other points of view is presented in what amounts mostly to a statement of beliefs.

NS (Nonscorable) No coherent claim, argument, or conclusion is presented.

Note: In standards documents, a simple tactic to help you identify valid criteria is to look at the adverbs and adjectives modifying the verbs in the standards (e.g., *thorough* explanation, *logical* reasoning, *sufficient* evidence) and construct rubrics explicitly around those criteria.

A second process for checking the criteria and rubric(s) in a unit is to use them to evaluate student work. Here is one protocol that can be used by an individual teacher or a team: Review student work and place the samples into four piles—excellent, good, fair, poor. As the student work is sorted, write down reasons for placing pieces in the various stacks. For example, if a selected work is placed in the excellent pile, describe its distinguishing features. What qualities differentiate this example from works of lesser quality? What makes this work stand out? What specific feedback might you offer a student as you return this work? Keep sorting the work until you cannot find anything new to add to a list of descriptors. The qualities you have identified are the most salient traits and reveal the key evaluative criteria.

See Problems #10 and #11 for related solutions.

(See Wiggins & McTighe, 2012, Modules J & M.)

Problems with the Learning Plan (Stage 3)

Problem #16. The proposed learning plan does not address the targeted understandings and essential questions.

Many units list one or more understandings and essential questions among their goals. However, the associated learning plan may not always do justice to them. It is easy to forget that the questions are meant to generate and focus ongoing inquiry. It is also easy to fall into the trap of merely "telling" the understandings instead of helping students deduce them. All too often, the big ideas—embodied in the questions and understandings—are merely presented by the teacher rather than serving as the grist for student "meaning-making."

Indicators of the failure to honor essential questions occur when the questions:

- Are merely posted on the board and occasionally referenced by the teacher, but there are no activities or assignments that ask students to use the questions to generate inquiries, connections, or responses.
- Are not addressed by students in either formative or summative assessments.
- Do not recur in texts, experiences, or issues that suggest a need to rethink previous answers.

- Are too numerous and therefore cannot be meaningfully addressed *throughout* the unit.

The learning plan fails to treat the desired understandings as key inferences to be drawn by students when the teacher:

- Posts understandings and may reference them, but students are not asked to draw conclusions on their own.
- Presents the understandings as if they were easy-to-grasp facts rather than hard-won inferences.
- Does not give students time to actively "make meaning"—no time is allocated for students to ponder, generate and test inferences, or to apply their learning to new situations.
- Allows students time to process what was learned, but their comments are merely accepted rather than analyzed and probed to ensure that they are appropriate and represent genuine understandings.

Here are suggestions for making essential questions a central strategy for developing and deepening students' understanding:

- Frame the unit's content around a few essential questions linked to big ideas that students should come to understand as important.
- Post the essential questions prominently in the classroom and regularly use them to interrogate each new text, activity, or experience.

- Require students to keep asking and answering the essential questions.
- Use the essential questions at the beginning of the unit as a pre-assessment and advanced organizer. Then, have students answer the questions as formative assessments to check their understanding.
- Use follow-up questions and probes, asking "Why?" "Tell me your thinking?" "Who disagrees with that?" "What evidence do you have to support your position?"
- Invite students to generate their own questions from the essential questions.

(See Wiggins & McTighe, 2011, Module H; Wiggins & McTighe, 2012, Module K.)

Problem #17. Unit does not include pre-assessments.

In some units, the learning plan (Stage 3) simply presents a sequential list of the content to be covered (sometimes with textbook chapters or page numbers cited) or a summary of the major learning activities for each lesson. Beginning with what the teacher will teach or what the students will do misses a vital component of effective learning—determining prior knowledge. The research on this matter could not be clearer: new learning is significantly influenced by what learners already know (or think they know). Accordingly, it is imperative for teachers to find out what students know or think they know and believe about a new topic, concept, or skill. Fortunately, there are several efficient pre-assessment techniques that can be used to uncover prior knowledge and skill levels. These include pre-tests, skill checks, K-W-L, and graphic representations.

A particularly valuable pre-assessment targets potential misconceptions. Research and experience have shown that some students come into school with prior knowledge in the form of misconceptions about subject matter (e.g., thinking that a heavier object will fall faster than a lighter one, or believing that if something is printed in a book, it must be true). It is critical that teachers uncover these erroneous ideas and address them instructionally. Failure to do so is likely to result in students layering new knowledge on top of a faulty foundation. Indeed, if teachers don't identify potential misconceptions, these erroneous ideas are likely to persist even in the face of good instruction.

Misconception checks can be efficiently presented at the start of a new unit (or lesson) as a set of statements or examples to which students must agree or disagree. Use methods such as true or false, thumbs up/thumbs down, or a student response system (a.k.a. clickers) that garner quick responses. The results provide invaluable information to help teachers target any prevailing misconceptions that need correction.

In sum, we strongly recommend that unit plans include appropriate pre-assessments, including checks for potential misconceptions—by design. The information gleaned through pre-assessments enables a teacher to decide the best starting place for instruction as well as to determine what differentiation may be needed to address variations in students' knowledge and skill levels. Indeed, if the goal is to maximize learning, then taking the time to pre-assess before introducing new content saves time in the long run because teachers can skip things that students already know and target things they don't yet understand.

See Problem #19 for a related solution.

(See Wiggins & McTighe, 2012, Module N.)

Problem #18. Unit plan fails to anticipate and check for possible or predictable misconceptions.

Educational research has long confirmed the critical role that prior knowledge plays in new learning. In recent years, greater attention is being paid to the recognition that learners often harbor predictable and persistent misconceptions and that these interfere with their understanding. Indeed, in spite of clear and focused teaching, students often persist in holding on to prior naïve conceptions.

Misconceptions exist in all subjects. Here are a few:

- An equals (=) sign means "find the answer."
- Authors always write what they mean.
- It's warmer in summer because the sun is closer to the earth.
- People in the past thought just the way we do.

Wise and experienced teachers anticipate and address misunderstandings in both formative assessment and throughout their learning plan. Failure to predict and assess misconceptions is evident when the unit plan:

- Does not offer opportunities to identify predictable misunderstandings.
- Does not include pre-assessments to diagnose potential misunderstandings.
- Does not include ongoing formative assessments to determine if students are overcoming their misunderstandings.
- Includes planned assessments that only test discrete facts and skills. Such assessments do not gauge whether students are overcoming common misunderstandings about the larger ideas of the topic.

Here are some tips for identifying and addressing predictable misconceptions in unit plans:

- Identify the most likely misconceptions or naïve ideas that students will bring to the unit. Target these in an ungraded pre-assessment prior to teaching, followed by a post-test to see if students have overcome them.
- Ask follow-up questions that are differently worded, less scaffolded, and/or that vary in setup to find out if students achieved the new understanding, as opposed to merely memorizing the answer for given examples.
- Search the Internet for lists of common misunderstandings and assessments that can be used to ferret them out (e.g., for science, see http://assessment.aaas.org/topics)

(See Wiggins & McTighe, 2012, Module N.)

Problem #19. Unit lacks ongoing formative assessments.

The purpose of formative assessment is to inform—to provide feedback to both teachers and learners about what is working and what adjustments are needed. Indeed, we know that feedback is essential for improvement and accomplishment—whether you are learning to ride a bicycle, trying to perfect a golf swing, cooking a new meal, or writing an article. Despite this awareness, we have seen too many unit plans in which there is no (or minimal) attention to formative assessments.

The reasons for omitting formative assessments are varied. Some teachers believe that they simply don't have enough time to assess along the way since there is so much material to cover. It may be that they never learned about formative assessment strategies in their teacher-prep program. Perhaps a few teachers believe that their job is only to "deliver" and the students' job is to "get it." Others may feel that giving the local interim or benchmark assessments are all they need. Regardless of the explanation, any series of lessons that omits formative assessments is missing a crucial dimension of effective instruction.

To rectify this omission, we encourage teachers to observe their colleagues in the performance-based subjects (e.g., the arts, physical education and athletics, and vocational-technical courses) and coaches and sponsors of extracurricular activities (e.g., athletics, band, newspaper, and debate). No successful athletic coach waits until the game to see how his or her team is doing and to make adjustments as warranted by the feedback. Indeed, the essence of coaching is giving continuous feedback to individual athletes and teams as they work to refine their skills and strategies during practices. Ongoing assessment and feedback during practice is the route to improved game performance—just as it should be in academic classrooms.

Assessing learning in progress can be done in a variety of ways, including teacher questioning, observing students while learning, and examining student work. Such ongoing assessments offer immediate feedback and let teachers know which students are struggling and which are excelling, and what adjustments are needed. Other approaches include hand signals, white boards, student response systems (a.k.a. clickers), exit slips, concept maps, and learning summaries. These kinds of assessment need to be part of the lesson plans and regularly employed. In other words, build in extra time for the assessment and use of the results to ensure that you don't feel like there is no time to adjust when needed. Because formative assessments are meant to *inform*, not evaluate, teachers should not factor formative assessment results into the calculation of a final grade.

Remember, formative assessments are meant to *inform* by providing feedback to teachers and students. To be effective, feedback needs to be timely, specific, and understandable to the learner. Here is a straightforward test: Based on your feedback, ask students to tell you specifically what they have done well and what they can do to improve. If they cannot tell you, then the feedback is not sufficiently specific or understandable enough for the student.

See Problems #10 and #16 for related solutions.

(See Wiggins & McTighe, 2012, Module N.)

Problem #20. Unit plan does not include time for needed adjustments.

Driven by the pressures to cover large amounts of content, teachers often design jam-packed units with little or no time allotted to address the nearly inevitable setbacks and unexpected interruptions. Anyone who has taught for more than a few months recognizes that unexpected interruptions (e.g., fire drills and snow days) as well as scheduled events (e.g., student assemblies and field trips) are likely to intrude on valuable instructional time. Moreover, even the best planned lessons and skillful instruction cannot ensure that every learner will get it. But without any built-in flex time, teachers feel great pressure to move on and are often reluctant to reteach what was not adequately learned. This problem is exacerbated when teachers are required to follow rigid pacing guides.

Indicators that there is insufficient flex time for needed adjustments include the following:

- Review of lesson indicates plans are made for every minute of every day during the unit.
- Introduction of a new topic despite assessment results that reveal persistent misunderstandings or key skill deficiencies.

- Survey of student expressions and body language indicate that some aren't getting it.
- Use of few or no revealing formative assessments; results are not being sufficiently considered for best next steps.
- Lack of reteaching or opportunities for students to try again.

As research and common sense make clear, good feedback and opportunities to use it is one of the highest yield approaches to achieve genuine understanding and lasting learning. So, resist the urge to press on if you desire high levels of learning by more students.

Our advice for addressing this problem is simple, yet powerful: allocate an unscheduled day or two within each unit where the sole purpose is to use formative results to make needed adjustments to enhance learning. (A teacher friend of ours describes this as building a "speed bump" into the curriculum.) By including adjustment time into your unit plan, you acknowledge the fluid nature of effective teaching and learning and avoid letting content coverage or imposed schedules dictate the flow of learning.

(See Wiggins & McTighe, 2012, Module O.)

Problem #21. The learning sequence is too linear and likely to bore or confuse learners.

We have seen some curriculum plans that show nothing more than a march through a textbook, chapter-by-chapter.

But stop for a minute and ponder: Is this the sequence most likely to be meaningfully engaging and lead to deep understanding? Is this the way that learning unfolds in athletics, in the arts, in engineering, in technology, in business? Do the most interesting books and movies follow such a course? Not likely. In sports, you don't merely learn rules and basic skills out of context for the first few years before you are allowed on the field to play the game. In art, you don't have to memorize the color wheel and learn about brushes until you are somehow ready to paint or draw. In all courses that go in-depth, you revisit key ideas and performance demands repeatedly—hence, the "spiral curriculum."

Unit plans that simply march through a body of knowledge, be it chapters in a textbook or a list of standards, thus reveal confusion about the proper sequencing of learning. Textbooks are organized by a logical sequence of topics, just as a dictionary and the how-to manual for your computer are organized, but you would not read them from cover to cover. You refer to them on an as-needed or as-interested basis to address a question or solve a problem.

The link between instructional sequence and engagement is clear. Students have for decades identified the arts, science (when taught in a "hands-on" manner), athletics, and technology as their favorite subjects. Why? Because the learners are immersed in using what they are learning right from the start. The most effective instruction is iterative, not linear; and students improve when they revisit important ideas, processes, and questions over time.

A learning sequence is not optimal when it is

- Organized by the topics to be covered.
- Linear—everything is covered once, step-by-step and superficially.
- Lockstep with the textbook, which is a generic resource like a dictionary or how-to manual.
- Inexplicable to (and by) students as to how learning flows from week to week.

If you recognize this problem in your own unit planning and teaching, we encourage you to experiment with varied approaches to sequence for better ways to hook students right away, help them see how one thing leads to another, and keep them interested and engaged throughout the unit. Here are some tips for rethinking sequence in order to cause more engagement and deeper learning:

- Begin the unit with a thought-provoking problem, activity, or experience that raises key issues.
- Return to the essential question(s) multiple times, after each chunk of content, to achieve greater coherence and depth with the unit.
- Watch a few documentary films to see how they pique viewers' interest and sustain that interest, and borrow some of the techniques. Hint: Think of your curriculum as telling a story as opposed to covering content.
- Think like a coach—be it of a sport or an extracurricular activity. Apply the typical sequence of coaching to your teaching plan. Almost every set of practices in a coaching situation mixes skill learning via modeling

and drills with immediate application involving authentic performance.

(See Wiggins & McTighe, 2011, Module H; Wiggins & McTighe, 2012, Module O.)

Problem #22. The learning plan does not adequately prepare students to transfer their learning.

In each unit plan, we encourage teachers to include one or more performance tasks that call for learners to transfer their learning to authentic situations. Typically, these tasks occur at, or near, the end of a unit and the results provide evidence of students' understanding and ability to apply their learning in a meaningful way. Ideally, teachers would then develop their day-to-day learning plans "backward" from the demands of the task(s).

Our experience is that this ideal does not always happen. Some teachers add an authentic performance task at the end of a unit, without changing their instruction whatsoever. In other words, the performance task is simply given to the class at the end of a unit without necessary preparation. Consider this analogy to athletics: Imagine if a coach only allowed players to work on isolated skills of the game and go over the rules, but never let them step onto the court or field until the day of the game. Predictably, their performance would be disappointing. Unfortunately, we have seen the equivalent in academic classes when teachers focus on covering content as they always have instead of preparing their students for complex performances.

Here are indicators that students lack adequate preparation for the unit performance task(s):

- Students perform poorly on tasks that call for transfer.
- Students have questions about how to do a task, especially, "What are we supposed to do?" "Is this what you want?"
- Students do not have the opportunity to engage in the complete task. Analogously, the players never have a scrimmage before they play a real game.

Think about how coaches of athletics and the arts prepare their students for authentic performances that involve transfer. These coaches do not simply teach and practice isolated skills nor do they expect the drills to transfer automatically to the game or performance. They engage players, artists, and students in scrimmages and dress rehearsals—simulations of the performance—in order to prepare them for the game, play, or recital. We encourage teachers to think like a coach and act accordingly.

Here are suggestions for developing and preparing students for transfer performances:

- Select or develop one or more performance tasks that require students to apply (transfer) their learning.
- Analyze the task for its requirements and teach the requisite knowledge, skills, and strategies. For example, what will students need to know? What skills are needed? What will they need to understand to perform well? What strategies will be important?

- Preview the culminating performance tasks with students so that they will know the expected performances. Show them the associated rubrics and models of performance so that they are clear about the expectations.
- Pre-assess students to determine their prior knowledge, skills, and understandings in light of the task requirements.
- Plan your teaching based on the knowledge, skills, and understandings that students will need for successful performance. Differentiate instruction as necessary based on the pre-assessment results.
- Present students with one or more minitasks— less complex or varied versions of the culminating performance tasks—and use them for guided practice with feedback.
- Allow students to practice with a similar task—the equivalent of a scrimmage in athletics or a dress rehearsal for theater or band—before encountering the real thing.

(See Wiggins & McTighe, 2011, Modules E & H; Wiggins & McTighe, 2012, Module N.)

Problem #23. The learning plan is not differentiated.

Some units present a standardized plan whereby all students learn the same thing in the same way on the same day. Although this may be efficient for the teacher, it is unlikely that a one-size-fits-all learning plan will be optimal for the variety of learners we serve. Indeed, most classes contain students with notable differences in their background experiences, prior knowledge, and skill levels. In some schools, significant cultural and gender differences may also be at play. Even in classes that are "ability grouped," the learners are likely to vary according to their interests and preferred methods of learning.

To accommodate differences and to better serve individual students, effective teachers differentiate their unit plans. A unit plan can be differentiated according to three dimensions: (1) Input—how the content is presented and accessed; (2) Process—the various learning activities and how students work; and (3) Products—what students produce as a result of their work on assignments and assessments.

Decisions about *what* and *how* to differentiate *for whom* can be made as a result of the information provided by pre-assessments and formative assessments. Thus, it is critical for teachers to build such assessments into their unit plans and use the information to tailor their instruction and assessment.

Although we want our curriculum plan to be responsive to the diverse learners we serve, not everything in a unit should be differentiated. As a general rule, we propose that identified standards should be the target for all learners (with the exception of students who have an Individualized Education Plan). We also recommend using the same essential questions for an entire class. However, since students typically vary in their prior knowledge and skill levels, some differentiation may be needed if and when pre-assessments reveal skill gaps or misconceptions.

The assessment evidence we need is derived from the identified unit goals and should not vary notably from student to student. However, the *particulars* of an assessment can be differentiated to accommodate the uniqueness of students as long as comparable evidence is obtained. For example, a student for whom English is not his or her home language may be unable to pass a written test on a science concept. However, that student may be able to display understanding of the concept if allowed to show it visually or to give an oral explanation.

Our recommendation to differentiate unit plans does not mean that a teacher is expected to individualize instruction to meet the unique needs and interests of every learner at all times. That would not be feasible for most teachers. Rather, we encourage teachers to tailor their unit plans in ways that are both manageable and likely to have the highest yield for the greatest number of learners.

(See Wiggins & McTighe, 2012, Module N.)

Problem #24. There is no plan for increasing student autonomy and transfer of learning.

The goal of education is not to simply learn things as presented by the teacher; the goal of education is autonomous transfer of learning—for students to be able to independently apply learning to new challenges, in and beyond school. Far too many students leave K–12 education without the ability to handle the novel and messy challenges that they will face in the world or to adapt prior learning to new challenges.

They have become so used to being told what to do and how to do it that they have no experience in handling genuine problems, inquiries, or challenges where no step-by-step path to a solution is evident. Just making the work harder and harder over the years spent in school does not touch this problem.

Indicators of a lack of a plan for increasing student autonomy and transfer:

- Poor student performance on novel tasks that require judgment and transfer of learning, despite doing well on prior tasks that were familiar, highly scaffolded, or directed.
- Little to no increase in student autonomy, choice, or self-directed learning over time, although the content of the unit and course may get more demanding.
- Minimal opportunities for students to use judgment and autonomy; assignments and assessments remain highly directed throughout the unit and course.

The phrase *gradual release of teacher responsibility* summarizes what needs to occur. Here's a four-stage protocol for the basic process for decreasing teacher guidance and increasing student autonomy: "I do, you watch; I do, you help; you do, I help; you do, I watch." The benefit is that the more students learn how to learn on their own, the better they do on standardized tests where teacher help, scaffolding, or reminders are not allowed.

Here are suggestions for developing and increasing student autonomy in learning:

- Design "backward" from the last unit of the year, when students will have to be completely self-directed and self-sufficient in handling a complex task at the heart of the course. Then, as you plan units throughout the year, mindfully and gradually release responsibility to your students as they develop the necessary skills of self-direction.
- Increase the number and length of lessons in which work has to be done independently as the year progresses.
- Use a rubric that describes how much teacher help was needed to complete a task; for example, completed independently with no teacher help; completed with just a few teacher reminders; completed with lots of teacher assistance; completed with step-by-step teacher guidance all along the way. Use the rubric with other rubrics, and alert students that over the course of the year, their goal is increasing autonomy and self-direction on complex tasks.

(See Wiggins & McTighe, 2011, Modules E & H; Wiggins & McTighe, 2012, Module N.)

Problem #25. The learning plan is not aligned with the goals and/or assessments.

One of the key characteristics of effective unit design is coherence; that is, all the units' components are in complete alignment. More specifically, the assessments provide valid evidence for all identified unit goals, and the lessons and learning events are well sequenced to help learners achieve the desired results. Moreover, the purpose and structure of the unit design should be clear to the learners. They should know the learning goals, why they matter, how their learning will be assessed, and the instructional pathway they will follow.

Checking for alignment and coherence within a unit is straightforward. Here are indicators that the unit design is incoherent and misaligned:

- Review of learning events reveals they do not align with identified goals or assessments.
- Review of lessons plans by colleagues reveals they cannot infer unit goals.
- Review of assessments by colleagues indicates they cannot infer unit goals.
- Comments by students show they cannot connect learning activities or explain the flow of past or future lessons.
- Questions from students include "Why are we doing this? Are we done yet?"

Our solutions to solving alignment and coherence issues within a unit are clear-cut. Try the following:

- Plan backward. Ask yourself: "*If* this is what I want students to know, understand, and be able to do, *then* what evidence do I need to see if students are attaining these outcomes?" Then, ask: "*If* this is what students will need to do to demonstrate their learning, *then* what learning experiences and instruction will they need to achieve these desired outcomes?"

- Code each of your unit's goals. For example, S1 for one skill; S2 for another, U1 for an understanding. Then, use the same codes when determining your assessment evidence. Alignment means that each targeted goal is being appropriately assessed. If you find lack of alignment, then you will need to either add one or more assessments or eliminate those goals for which you will collect no evidence.
- Use the same codes as for your learning goals and code each learning event in your lesson plans to ensure connections to those goals and the associated assessments. Make necessary adjustments.
- Ask for regular feedback from your students. Do they understand the goals and priorities for their learning in this unit? Can they explain what they will do to show their learning? Do they see the flow of the learning activities?
- Ask your students for suggestions for improvement the next time you teach the unit. Their feedback can be invaluable in helping you better align and refine your unit plans.

(See Wiggins & McTighe, 2011, Module K; Wiggins & McTighe, 2012, Modules O & P.)

References

Wiggins, G., & McTighe, J. (2011). *The Understanding by Design Guide to Creating High-Quality Units*. Alexandria, VA: ASCD.

Wiggins, G., & McTighe, J. (2012). *The Understanding by Design Guide to Advanced Concepts in Creating and Reviewing Units*. Alexandria, VA: ASCD.

Related Resources

Essential Questions: Opening Doors to Student Understanding by Jay McTighe and Grant Wiggins (#109004)

Integrating Differentiated Instruction and Understanding by Design: Connecting Content and Kids by Carol Ann Tomlinson and Jay McTighe (#105004)

Making the Most of Understanding by Design by John L. Brown (#103110)

Schooling by Design: Mission, Action, and Achievement by Grant Wiggins and Jay McTighe (#107018)

Understanding by Design expanded 2nd edition by Grant Wiggins and Jay McTighe (#103055)

Understanding by Design Guide to Advanced Concepts in Creating and Reviewing Units by Grant Wiggins and Jay McTighe (#112026)

Understanding by Design Guide to Creating High-Quality Units by Grant Wiggins and Jay McTighe (#109107)

The Understanding by Design Professional Development Workbook by Jay McTighe and Grant Wiggins (#103056)

About the Authors

Jay McTighe brings a wealth of experience developed during a rich and varied career in education. He served as director of the Maryland Assessment Consortium, a state collaboration of school districts working together to develop and share formative performance assessments. Prior to this position, Jay was involved with school improvement projects at the Maryland State Department of Education where he directed the development of the Instructional Framework, a multimedia database on teaching. Jay is well known for his work with thinking skills, having coordinated statewide efforts to develop instructional strategies, curriculum models, and assessment procedures for improving the quality of student thinking. In addition to his work at the state level, Jay has experience at the district level in Prince George's County, Maryland, as a classroom teacher, resource specialist, and program coordinator. He also directed a state residential enrichment program for gifted and talented students. Contact information: Jay McTighe, 6581 River Run, Columbia, MD 21044-6066 USA. E-mail: jmctigh@aol.com.

 **Grant Wiggins** is president of Authentic Education in Hartford, Connecticut. He earned his EdD from Harvard University and his BA from St. John's College in Annapolis. Grant and his colleagues consult with schools, districts, and state and national education departments on a variety of reform matters. He and his colleagues also organize conferences and workshops, and develop print and web resources on key school reform issues. Grant may be contacted at gwiggins@authenticeducation.org.